Ellie and Sam

Written by Claire Llewellyn

Illustrated by Sarah Warburton

Ellie and Sam
like going to school.

2
4

Ellie likes reading.

Sam does too.

Ellie likes painting.

Sam does too.

Ellie likes writing.

Sam does too.

Ellie likes lunch time.

Sam does too.

Ellie likes water.

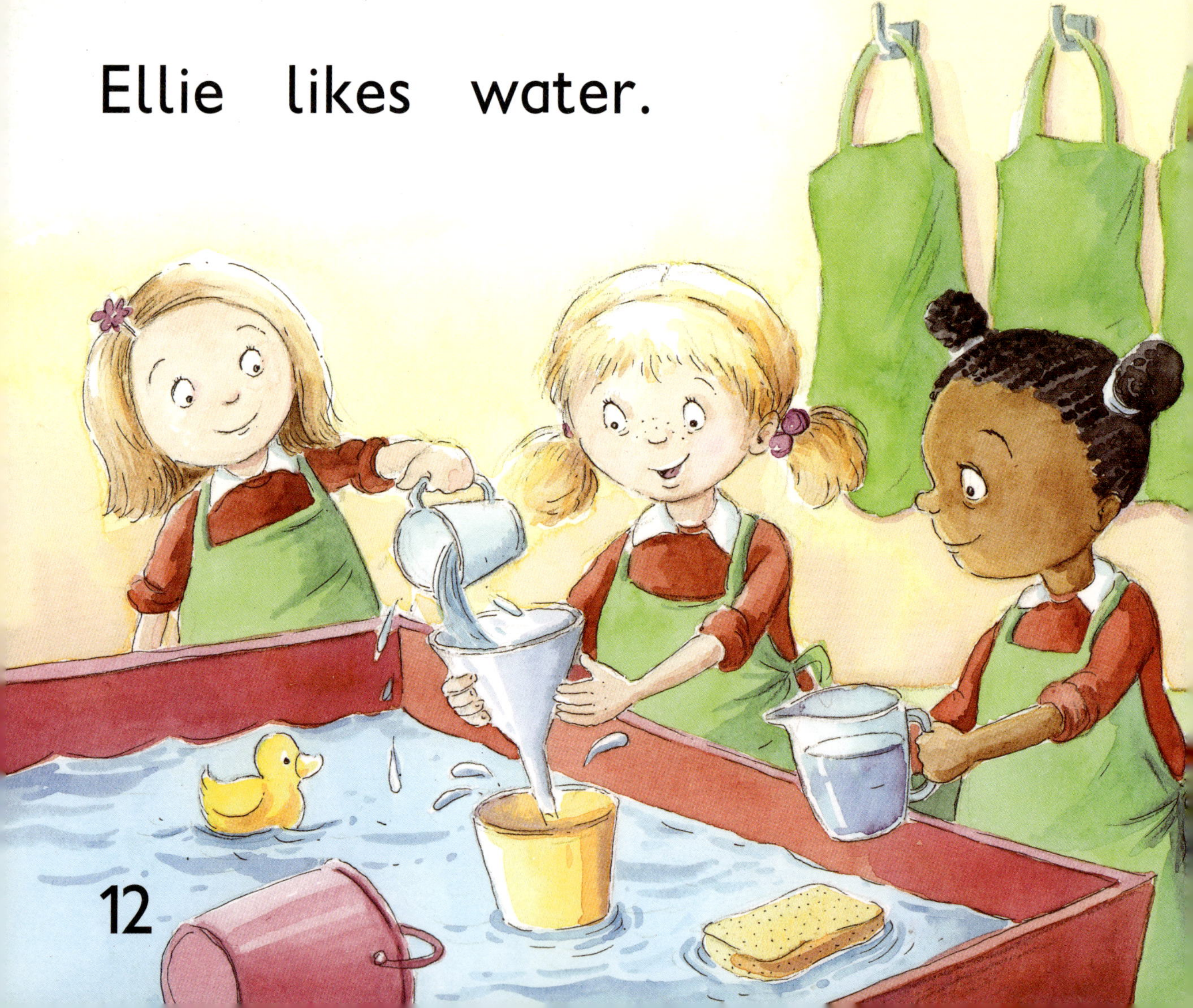

Sam does too.

Ellie likes football.

Sam does too.

Ellie likes Sam.

Sam likes Ellie.